Beethoven

By Lene Mayer-Skumanz
Illustrated by Winfried Opgenoorth

Translated by Alexis L. Spry

NorthSouth BOOKS

New York / London

NAMED FOR HIS GRANDFATHER, Ludwig van Beethoven would far surpass the passion and talent of the elder man. His grandfather, coming from a long line of farmers, was the first Beethoven to earn his living as a musician, singer, and court composer in the noble city of Bonn, Germany.

Standing beneath his grandfather's portrait, the cherubic child remembered his lovely, deep voice and being bounced on his knee to the rhythm of a song. He was most comfortable when he was surrounded by music. The younger Beethoven would go to the piano, climb onto the stool, and tentatively press a few keys, while peering at the doorway. His father didn't like it when Ludwig played the notes that he heard in his head instead of those in his music book. And if he didn't practice the music in his book enough, he'd get his ears boxed.

Beethoven listened. It was quiet in the apartment, except for the sound of a baby crying. Out in the yard, he could hear the Fischers' children playing. Their parents owned the house on Rheingasse in Bonn.

Unable to earn enough as a singer, Beethoven's father was forced to give music lessons to the rich. His grandfather, too, despite reaching the level of court composer, had to earn money on the side as a wine seller and had died when little Beethoven was three years old. His grandmother was still alive, but no one spoke of her much. Too much wine had made her sick, and she was taken care of by the nuns. That was why Beethoven's mother always worried about his father and his fondness for wine. Despite this, she would still buy wine for him—especially on days when he brought money home. Beethoven never saw his mother yell. But he never saw her happy, either.

Beethoven took up his violin and played a melody that he'd made up for his grandfather's portrait. His grandfather had always loved the violin. Suddenly, the door burst open.

"What kind of horrible screeching is that?" cried his father. "Just play the notes in your books!"

Beethoven looked at his father and then at the portrait of his grandfather. Tentatively, he played his melody once more. "Don't you think it sounds nice?"

"That's not real music," shouted his father. "Play the notes in your book!" He raised his hand threateningly.

BEETHOVEN'S FATHER was strict and rough with him, yet among his music colleagues he was always so cheerful. Sometimes if he'd had too much to drink, he would stumble into the children's room in the middle of the night and tear Beethoven from his bed. "You have to practice!" He desperately wanted Beethoven to be a child prodigy like Mozart had been. When Beethoven was eight years old, his father had him play the piano at a concert and lied about his age. The program said he was six.

His father's musician friends worried about the little one. He was always so serious—and so shy! His father's unrealistic expectations were sure to harm him. So the friends started teaching Beethoven to play the violin, piano, and organ. Soon, he could play the organ so well that, at age ten, he replaced his teacher at the early morning mass—unpaid, of course. His classmates in school didn't notice anything special about him, except that he was often dirty and unkempt.

The new court organist, Christian Gottlob Neefe, was the teacher who would most influence Beethoven. Under him, Beethoven learned to play works of Bach and composed his own pieces. Best of all, he could talk to this teacher about anything. Neefe believed that music was a special form of art that made people better and smarter. He taught the young Beethoven the importance of reading and learning. To encourage him, he had Beethoven's first big compositions printed. He even wrote the following about his student in a magazine: "He will certainly become a second Wolfgang Amadeus Mozart if he continues to make such progress. He should be supported and allowed to travel..."

But at the time, traveling was not an option. Beethoven had to help support his family. The new Archbishop and Elector Maximilian Franz employed the 14-year-old Beethoven as a court musician and paid him for his services as organist and harpsichordist during opera performances. Beethoven understood what was expected of him and knew that he could no longer run around in tattered clothing. He wore a tailcoat and short green pants, white silk stockings, a flowered silk vest embellished with golden embroidery, and carried a small sword under his left arm.

Suddenly, for the first time, he was making friends, including Franz Wegeler, who would become a lifelong friend. Working as a piano teacher for the von Breuning family, Beethoven met the siblings Leonore and Stephan. Their mother, Helene von Breuning, treated the young musician as her own child. Beethoven was happy in his circle of friends.

When he was 17 he received a stipend to study in Vienna. His friends were happy for him. Perhaps he would meet Mozart. But Beethoven was only able to stay in Vienna for three weeks. A letter from his father brought him back to Bonn in despair. His mother was on her deathbed.

Broke, he had to borrow money to get home. Despite his rush, he made a stop in Augsburg to visit the famous instrument maker Andreas Stein and his daughter Nanette. Nanette was thrilled when he tried out her father's pianos.

While he played, his fears subsided—but only while he played. A few days after his return, his mother died, and Ludwig van Beethoven was left to take care of his two younger brothers and his alcoholic father. He alone supported the family financially.

Luckily, his friends stuck by him, and he became well known as a pianist. Not only could he play any music provided, but he could create variations on it—variations so new and powerful that they took the audience's breath away.

Once, he was playing the organ in a church that was being renovated. The audience in the organ loft was deeply moved. The workers below laid down their shovels, one by one. They were astounded by what they heard. What music this was! They would never forget it as long as they lived.

At 19, BEETHOVEN enrolled at the University of Bonn. He learned to think critically and to form his own opinions. Like a hungry wolf gulping down a meal, Beethoven devoured lectures, political texts, and books.

In Paris, France, the citizens had stormed a prison, started a revolution, and abolished the nobility. On August 27, 1789, the Declaration of the Rights of Man was proclaimed. Beethoven liked these democratic ideals of liberty, equality, and fraternity, and he liked the idea that the people should rule, rather than royalty.

One of Beethoven's favorite professors at the university was Professor Fischenich, and he enjoyed his lectures on Greek poetry, natural justice, and human rights. Fischenich was a friend of the poet Friedrich von Schiller and he often read Schiller's poetry to his students. One such poem was Schiller's "Ode to Joy."

Although Beethoven's childhood had been unhappy, he strongly believed that joy was something everyone needed. And so he decided that he must set this poem to music. This would be no simple song, but something special—a piece that would unite the orchestra with the choir and show listeners that a loving human community was a dream that could be fulfilled! It was a plan that would haunt Beethoven for most of his life.

If only he could go back to Vienna! Mozart had already passed away, but perhaps the famous Joseph Haydn would be a good teacher for him. But Beethoven worried about leaving his family. His brother Kaspar Karl was educated as a musician, and the other brother Nikolaus Johann was a pharmacist's apprentice. He could do nothing more for his father, who would eventually

drink himself to death.

Vienna was the right place for a glamorous musical career, and Beethoven's friends agreed. Finally, in the fall of 1792, it was time. His friend Count Waldstein helped him secure a stipend to study in Vienna. He took care of the travel expenses and introduced Beethoven to the Viennese nobility. Friends wrote their good luck wishes in Beethoven's journal.

Not everyone was happy to see Beethoven leave. The saddest was Leonore von Breuning, who wrote a proverb about lifelong friendship into the book. But how should she sign it? "From your friend and classmate Lorchen," as she'd always signed his birthday cards? Did Beethoven realize how much she liked him? Of course he did, but he wasn't ready to make a commitment. He wanted to be free.

In the end she wrote: "Your true friend Leonore." She'd always be his friend, even after she married Beethoven's friend Wegeler. And Beethoven's heart would always race whenever he heard the name "Leonore."

On November 2, during a time of great turmoil, the 22-year-old Beethoven left his home. The army of the French Revolution had already conquered the left bank of the Rhine and was dangerously close to Bonn. The German troops were withdrawing. Anyone who could afford to fled.

The driver of Beethoven's coach sped like a madman straight through the ranks of the Hessian Army. Afterward, when they were safe, everyone tipped him generously. When Beethoven arrived in Vienna his wallet was light once more. Four weeks later his father died, and this time, Beethoven did not return home.

THE VIENNESE NOBILITY liked the young pianist and admired his powerful, expressive music. Prince Carl Lichnowsky brought Beethoven to his home, introduced him to his guests, and commissioned new pieces for his string quartet. But Beethoven didn't feel comfortable as a royal pianist. He had to obediently show up each day at three-thirty, well dressed and freshly shaven. "I can't keep this up!" he whined.

Despite this, Beethoven was happy that the prince loved music. The city of Bonn had been occupied by the French, and his sponsor there could no longer pay Beethoven's stipend. Lichnowsky jumped into the role of sponsor and employer. Beethoven moved into an apartment, rented a horse, and hired a servant. He took classes from Joseph Haydn, as well as from Albrechtsberger, the cathedral's resident composer and conductor, and from the Italian composer Salieri. All three found him to be a headstrong and stubborn student.

Beethoven gave piano lessons, too. In his first years in Vienna he composed Piano Sonata No. 3 in C Major, which he dedicated to Haydn, and Three Trios for Piano, Violin and Cello dedicated to Lichnowsky. He was commissioned to write dance music, minuettes, and German dances, which the Viennese loved. In 1796 he went on a concert tour of Prague, Dresden, and Berlin. He would have been very happy—were it not for something very strange and disturbing. He had begun to hear loud, high-pitched noises and tones that hurt his ears. They were so persistent that they sometimes made it impossible for him to hear high notes.

With a notebook full of ideas he returned to Vienna. He let off steam at the piano, composing the devilishly difficult piece Rondo a Capriccio for Piano in G Major (op. 129). But he also came up with some simple love songs.

Beethoven was again responsible for his brothers, who had joined him in Vienna. He helped them find work. But Beethoven's worries about the political situation began to cause him stomach trouble. Despite the feeling of revolution in the air, there was still no trace of freedom or equality. "I think," wrote Beethoven after two years in Austria, "that as long as the Austrians have their beer and sausages, they won't revolt."

In 1799 he received an unexpected guest. The Hungarian Countess Brunswick arrived at the top of his narrow winding stairs,

gasping for air with her two young daughters in tow. They wanted to spend their vacation in Vienna taking lessons with Beethoven. At first Beethoven refused. But Countess Therese, the older sister, had brought a music book along—Beethoven's Piano Trio, op. 1. She sat down at the piano and began to play. She sang the accompanying melody for violin or cello. Beethoven was delighted. Then it was the younger and prettier sister Josephine's turn. Beethoven promised to come to their hotel for daily piano lessons. Sometimes the lessons lasted for hours, while the hotel staff was forced to wait to serve lunch. The young countesses beamed. Mr. van Beethoven fussed over them and bent

their fingers over the keys so that they learned to hold their hands correctly.

Beethoven was appalled when their mother arranged an engagement for the 19-year-old Josephine with the much older Count Deym. The wedding would take place in Hungary. Beethoven brought her a farewell gift—variations for piano for fours hands on the song *Ich Denke Dein*. Josephine cried. Around this time, Beethoven composed many sad melodies.

One year later Beethoven had become so famous that he held his own concert in the Imperial Court Theater. For the first time the audience heard Beethoven's First Symphony in C Major, op. 21.

"FEEL LIKE A STROLL, Mr. van Beethoven?" the vintner asked amiably. "Should I bring you some hot milk with honey afterward? There's a cold wind today."

Beethoven stared at her with a furrowed brow. What was she whispering? "I'm fine," he grumbled, trudging down the well-worn path along the vineyard. The wind blew in his face. Beethoven could feel it, cold and sharp. But he couldn't hear it. The roaring in his ears was louder. He stopped, turned around, and looked over the cliff. He saw the church of Heiligenstadt, the village square, and the vintner's house in the October sun. It was a lovely, quiet place, far from the city of Vienna. Beethoven had lived here for six months and was working on his Second Symphony.

"You need to rest in the country," his doctor recommended. "It will be good for your hearing."

In the country, Beethoven lived as a hermit, alone with his music. People thought he was hostile, stubborn—even a people-hater! They weren't nice to him. But he loved people and desperately needed friends with whom he could speak openly. But he had to constantly tell people to speak louder—or even yell, because he couldn't hear them clearly.

He had lived with this pain for years, and it kept getting worse. When the Countess Giulietta Guicciardi looked at him tenderly and—with closed eyes—whispered a tender phrase, he could only guess what she said. He had to read her lips, as he had a year ago, when he dedicated a piano sonata to her.

He brought her miniature portrait with him to Heiligenstadt. He liked to look at it, her dark eyes, the curls on her forehead . . . Not being able to hear the words of those you loved was a torture that Beethoven could never describe. I'll die, he thought. Again and again he thought about suicide.

"Look out, sir!" a voice cried out.

Confused, Beethoven looked up. A shepherd boy was driving his flock down the path. Beethoven moved to the side of the road. The boy smiled at him. He brought his flute to his lips. What a strange picture: the shepherd's flute, the boy's fingers, his pursed lips, the silent song.

To Beethoven, the high tones of his flute were inaudible, and he had barely heard the boy's loud warning cry. He looked past the herd. Melodies jingled and jangled inside his head. He could hear *them* clearly. The music in his head had nothing to do with the sickness in his ears. God, he thought, you made me for composing. I live

for music. Give me strength.

He wrote a letter to his brothers, Karl and Johann—a letter that would be found and published after his death. In it, he explained his hopeless condition and his pain. At least after his death people would be able to understand and forgive him for his "hostile" ways. He was living proof that despite the odds, one can bravely persevere and become a worthy artist and human being.

It took Beethoven more than a day to write this letter, which would also become his will. He pressed his seal to the last page. "Heiligenstadt, October 10, 1802, thus do I take my farewell of thee—and indeed sadly . . ."

Yellow leaves waved outside his window. His hopes, like these leaves, dried up and blew away in the cold wind. Would God ever send him another day of joy? Humans needed joy to live. He certainly couldn't live without hope and joy. That would be too painful!

BEETHOVEN FELT THAT HIS PIANO playing touched and healed people. They felt comforted, reassured, and strengthened by his music. Some even broke out in tears. Sometimes Beethoven smiled when he thought about the sobbing and sniffling audience, but he knew that his music helped people to believe in goodness, truth, and beauty. Through his music, he hoped to help create a new world. Beethoven intently followed the world's progress towards freedom. In Russia, Czar Alexander I called for social reforms. This pleased Beethoven, and he dedicated Three Sonatas for Piano and Violin to him.

Several years earlier in France, General Napoleon Bonaparte had been named First Consul of the new republic. He was the victor in the wars against Austria. Beethoven was impressed with him and dedicated his latest symphony, his third, to his hero. The symphony was about a man and his strong feelings of love and pain. Beethoven wrote "For Bonaparte" on the title page.

By 1804, Beethoven was ready to practice the heroic piece. Prince Lobkowitz allowed him to use his palace and orchestra. He wanted to keep the symphony to himself for a while and enjoy it only with his private guests. Later it would be heard by the public. For this exclusivity, he paid Beethoven handsomely.

Beethoven accepted the money, but felt guilty about it. Shouldn't art be available to everyone—especially the poor? Again, Beethoven was plagued by stomach and intestinal pains, cramps, and diarrhea. He was very irritable. He argued with his friend von Breuning, who was kind enough to take care of him, and he threatened to box the ears of his cooperative piano student Ferdinand Ries. He was especially upset with Prince Lobkowitz. During a rehearsal, Lobkowitz thought the introduction of the horns at the end of a movement was a mistake and threatened the musicians with a cane. That night Beethoven refused to eat with the prince. Instead he chose to brood at a tavern. On the way home he shouted at the palace: "Lobkowitz, you are a donkey, Lobkowitz, you are an idiot!"

At the end of May 1804, his student Ferdinand Ries arrived with the news that

Napoleon had become the emperor of France!

Beethoven couldn't believe it: "Consul Bonaparte? Emperor?"

"Yes. And he crowned himself!"

"So he's no different from the rest," yelled Beethoven. "Now he will trample on the rights of man and live to fulfill his own ambition! He will become a tyrant!" Angrily he stormed to his table, where the score of *Eroica* lay. Beethoven ripped off the first page with the dedication and threw it on the ground. The page would be rewritten later— with the title *Eroica* Symphony.

New melodies were gathering in Beethoven's head. They appeared on their own, in the forest, on walks, in the stillness of the night. The tones rang, rushed, and stormed inside of him. He jotted them down. Along with an eerie, threatening knocking: *Ta-ta-ta-taaaaa*. What was that knocking on the door of his soul? Fate?

USING A FRENCH MODEL, the writer Josef Sonnleithner wrote a libretto for Beethoven. In the summer of 1805, Beethoven finished composing the opera in the open air of the quiet village of Hetzendorf, near the gates of Vienna. Sitting in the boughs of an oak tree, he felt like he was sitting between heaven and earth. The days—despite the warlike world affairs—were wonderfully peaceful, and he captured the "nameless joy" of the lovers in an opera named *Leonore*.

This is the story of a young woman named Leonore, searching for her husband, Florestan, who has disappeared. She suspects that Pizarro the magistrate is keeping him a prisoner. She disguises herself as the assistant jailer and calls herself Fidelio.

Leonore discovers her half-starved husband in the deepest dungeon just as Pizarro prepares to kill him. Pizarro knows that Don Fernando, Florestan's powerful friend, is on his way to inspect the prison. In haste, Pizarro raises his gun to shoot Florestan. Leonore jumps between them, grabs the pistol, and cries: "First kill his wife!"

At that moment, trumpets sound: "The minister has arrived!" Pizarro is arrested and the prisoners are freed. True love prevails as Leonore and Florestan are happily reunited.

But the time was not right for an opera premiere. The Viennese were worried about war and starvation. One week before the premiere, Napoleon's troops had moved into Vienna. There was hardly a house that wasn't filled with French soldiers. Who felt like going to the theater? Many French officers went out of sheer boredom, even though they barely understood German. Perhaps it would be a comedy. Or maybe there'd be ballet. They were very disappointed by the opera *Leonore*. The next night, the theater was empty.

Disappointed, but undaunted, Beethoven continued to work on his Fifth Symphony, written in C Minor with that eerie knocking at the beginning, and on the Sixth Symphony, which he called the *Pastoral* Symphony, the symphony about enjoying life in the country.

SPRING 1810 IN VIENNA. Beethoven stood at the window of his apartment on the fifth floor of the Pasqualati House on Mölker-bastei Street. From here, he could see over the inner city to the villages and vineyards in the northwest and to the Viennese woods. What an amazing view.

Beethoven took on a new piano student, Therese, the niece of his physician and friend Malfatti, and soon he fell in love. Therese was 21 years younger than he was. She was talented and emotive but her technique needed improvement. For her, he composed an easy-to-play, exhilarating piece in A Minor, and on the cover he wrote "For Therese."

Beethoven would do a lot "for Therese." He spent money on new suits, shirts, and scarves, because he wanted to improve his appearance for her.

Luckily, his royal friends, Archduke Rudoph, Prince Lobkowitz, and Prince Kinsky, had given him a stipend to keep him in Vienna and to prevent him from taking offers from foreign princes. With this money, Beethoven had enough to start his own family.

His friend Gleichenstein would present Therese's family with Beethoven's marriage proposal. He waited anxiously for their decision.

He ran to the bedroom, splashed cold water on his face, and took his time getting dressed. He tied his new scarf. How did it look? Where was his mirror? Then it occurred to him that he'd broken it at some point. Beethoven laughed in excitement. He sent a messenger with a short letter to his friend Nikolaus von Zmeskall, the cellist. "Could I please borrow the mirror that's hanging next to your window?"

Therese's parents rejected the marriage proposal, and Beethoven was devastated. Never again would he expect anything from other people. "That's it!" he wrote to Gleichenstein.

"Alas, poor Beethoven, you can't expect to find happiness from outside. You'll have to find happiness from within."

Beethoven holed up in his apartment, read poetry by Goethe, and set some to music. He didn't care what he or his apartment looked like.

One day pretty young Bettina von Brentano arrived at the filthy apartment. Not only was she the sister of a poet, she was also engaged to one, and it was her first time in Vienna. She was curious about the famous composer. Familiar with Beethoven's music, she yearned to learn more about him.

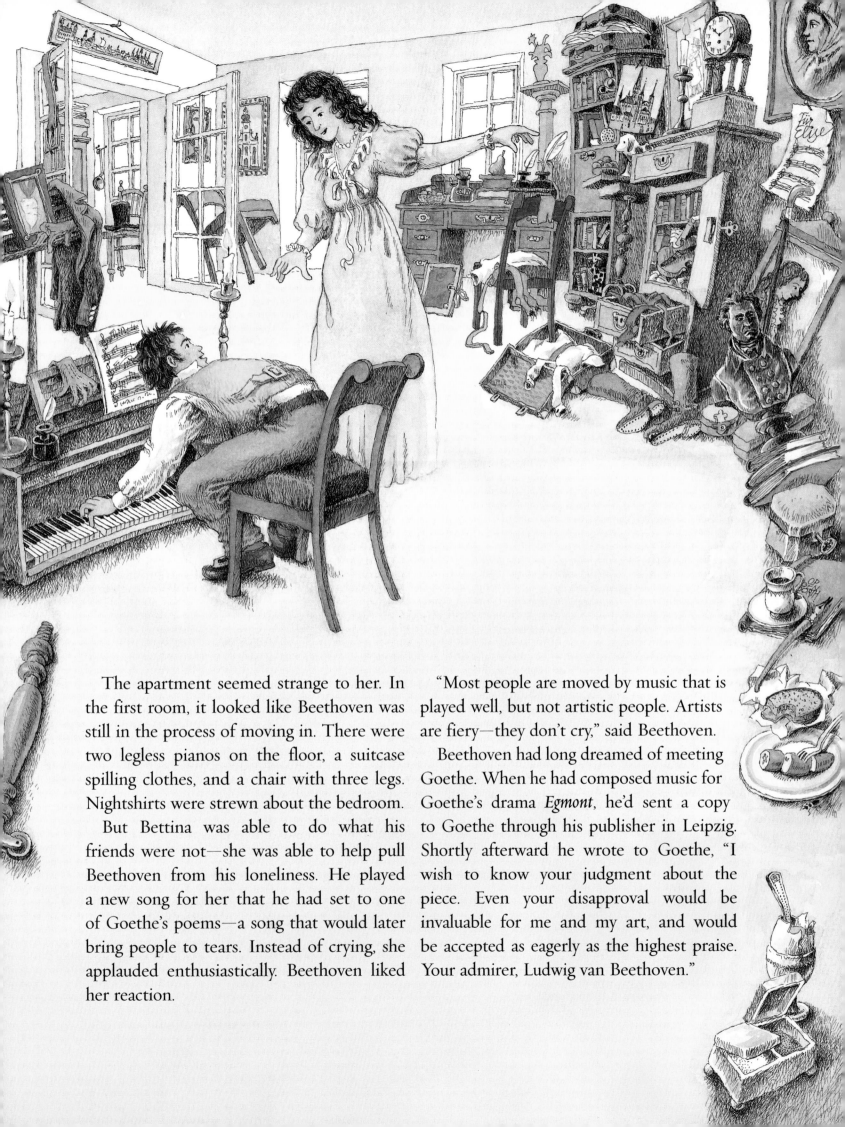

The apartment seemed strange to her. In the first room, it looked like Beethoven was still in the process of moving in. There were two legless pianos on the floor, a suitcase spilling clothes, and a chair with three legs. Nightshirts were strewn about the bedroom.

But Bettina was able to do what his friends were not—she was able to help pull Beethoven from his loneliness. He played a new song for her that he had set to one of Goethe's poems—a song that would later bring people to tears. Instead of crying, she applauded enthusiastically. Beethoven liked her reaction.

"Most people are moved by music that is played well, but not artistic people. Artists are fiery—they don't cry," said Beethoven.

Beethoven had long dreamed of meeting Goethe. When he had composed music for Goethe's drama *Egmont*, he'd sent a copy to Goethe through his publisher in Leipzig. Shortly afterward he wrote to Goethe, "I wish to know your judgment about the piece. Even your disapproval would be invaluable for me and my art, and would be accepted as eagerly as the highest praise. Your admirer, Ludwig van Beethoven."

Bettina was a close friend of Goethe's, and she arranged for Beethoven to meet him in the Bohemian spa of Teplitz.

Since the war with France, Austrian currency had lost a fifth of its value, and Beethoven's stipend was worth much less. He begged his sponsors to increase his salary. But Archduke Rudolph took his time responding and Prince Lobkowitz declined. His extravagance had depleted his finances. Even Prince Kinsky's treasurer denied an increase.

Still, Beethoven composed diligently. His Seventh Symphony was finished, and he had begun working on his Eighth Symphony.

Before he went to Teplitz for his meeting with Goethe, he stopped to visit Prince Kinsky in Prague. There was a motive behind his visit, and Prince Kinsky understood immediately. Of course he would raise Beethoven's stipend. Apologizing for the stubbornness of his treasurer, he gave Beethoven an advance. The stop in Prague had paid off!

Something else awaited Beethoven in Prague—a surprise sighting of the woman that Beethoven liked more than any of his friends, students, and admirers. She gave him a pencil. The pencil, and the memory of some unforgettable hours with her, inspired Beethoven's to write a letter to his "immortal beloved" while at an inn in Teplitz. On the chance that the letter might fall into the wrong hands, however, he never mentioned her name.

"My angel, my all, my very self!" There was so much that he wanted to share with her, but he realized that words could not adequately convey his emotions. Despite all the love he felt for her, he understood that she would never completely belong to him, nor he to her. And even if they couldn't have a life together—he vowed his devotion to her for all eternity. He saw their love as a heavenly structure . . . "Ever thine, ever mine, ever ours!" He wrote this letter in three parts and sent it on the morning of July 7.

A few days later Beethoven met Goethe. He played the piano for him and accompanied him on walks. But he refused to accompany him to parties hosted by the young emperor—first of all, because of his hearing problems, but also because he simply couldn't stand the people at court. Goethe, however, clearly enjoyed the royal air more than Beethoven expected—in fact, he thought Goethe enjoyed it a little too much!

One day Beethoven and Goethe were strolling arm in arm and they came across the emperor and his royal entourage. Goethe hurriedly pulled away from Beethoven. He wanted to make room for the royals, as was the custom. But Beethoven held tightly on to

Goethe. "Stay together with me," he growled. "They should be making room for us, not us for them!" But Goethe tore himself free, jumped to the side of the street, took his hat from his head, and bowed deeply. He bowed again and again.

Unfazed, Beethoven strolled on, lifting his hat a little. The royal entourage parted, made room for him, and greeted him amiably. Then they moved back together. Beethoven waited for Goethe, shaking his head. "You see, I'm waiting for you because I respect y ou, and you've earned this respect. But you've honored them too much!"

Beethoven and Goethe were not going to become good friends. Beethoven understood this. He also understood that the spa in Teplitz was not helping him. His hearing was getting worse and his stomach pains had begun again.

And his immortal beloved, she had returned his letter. She, too, was afraid it would fall into the wrong hands. Beethoven didn't know what to do with the letter. He didn't want to throw it away because it had been in her hands, on her cheek, at her bosom. He locked the letter in a drawer where it remained until his death.

FOR EIGHT YEARS, none of Beethoven's operas were performed. *Leonore* had been a failure. Perhaps it was too long and too difficult? His best friend Stephan von Breuning had shortened the piece but the abridgement didn't help. The Austrian army had been defeated at Austerlitz and misery and destitution had crept into Vienna. The Viennese didn't want to see suffering people at the opera—they were surrounded by suffering in real life.

By 1814, times had changed. Napoleon had been defeated and lived in exile on the island of Elba. Operas that had been popular in Paris were no longer stylish in Vienna. The managers of the Imperial Theater now wanted a performance of the opera *Leonore*. Those who worked backstage in the theater believed that Beethoven's opera would be a great success.

Beethoven asked the director of the Kärntnertor Theater, Georg Friedrich von Treitschke, to write a new libretto for one of Florestan's arias, which emphasized the thirst for freedom and hope. At first, von Treitschke hesitated. He would try his best.

But would a half-starved prisoner, chained in total darkness, sitting in his own filth, still have the strength to hope and to sing? Von Treitschke wrote several versions, but Beethoven wasn't satisfied with any of them.

He insisted that something strong, arousing, auspicious was needed. Von Treitschke would try to talk Beethoven out of this crazy idea over a nice dinner. Mrs. von Treitschke agreed and quickly invited a few friends to join them.

In order not to anger Beethoven, von Treitschke prepared a few scribbled verses on a piece of paper. An angel would appear to the dying Florestan, who was half-crazed from fear and hunger—an angel with the face of his wife!

As soon as he arrived, Beethoven read the hastily written lines.

"And do I not feel soft whispering air? What brightness shines into my grave? I see an angel fragrant as a rose, comforting, she stands by my side. An angel, Leonora, so like my wife, to lead me to freedom, to the kingdom of God!"

Beethoven forgot to take off his hat and stumbled toward the piano.

"Mr. van Beethoven, the soup is served!"

But Beethoven heard nothing about soup. Instead, he heard Florestan painfully putting his hope in a heavenly being.

"But, Mr. van Beethoven, the roast—won't you at least have a little dessert?"

Beethoven moaned, groaned, and pounded feverishly at the piano.

The guests didn't dare disturb him, and

waited patiently for him to awaken from his creative streak.

Mrs. von Treitschke said in her gentlest voice: "Should the maid—"

"Thank you," sniffed Beethoven. "That was delicious. I must go home quickly to write the aria."

"But the food!"

"Oh, it was excellent!"

The Viennese audiences applauded the opera now called *Fidelio*.

In the fall, audiences also applauded in Prague. And in Dresden and in Berlin.

DAY-TO-DAY LIFE WAS EXHAUSTING for Beethoven. His house was a mess and there were rarely any clean clothes.

"Riffraff!" shouted Beethoven at his servants.

Beethoven was lucky to have Nanette Streicher. As a young woman in Augsburg, she had adored his piano playing. Now she lived in Vienna and was married to the piano maker Andreas Streicher. She helped Beethoven with his rundown household. She'd speak patiently with cooks and maids on behalf of the deaf, distrustful composer, who shoved paper and pencils at his visitors for lengthy "conversations." Countless "conversation notebooks" would be written by friends, volunteers, and by "secretaries" like Anton Schindler, the Viennese poet Franz Grillparzer, with whom Beethoven wanted to write a libretto, and by Beethoven's

nephew Karl. After the death of his brother, Beethoven had assumed the guardianship of Karl. He spent a lot of his money on the boy, paying for tutors and boarding school.

It was not easy to live as a freelance artist in Vienna. If he couldn't depend on the nobility, he would have to depend on the taste of the public. Beethoven thought of his art as being willful, going in new directions, always progressing. But he still had to write pieces that would have mass appeal. He called it lowering himself to the common man. To gain the time and money for a new piece, I first must please the masses, he thought.

He was working on two large pieces—pieces that would set the standard. One was a mass for His Royal Highness, Archduke Rudolph, whom he had been teaching for years. And the other was his latest symphony, his Ninth—which would feature Schiller's

"Ode to Joy," sung by a huge choir!

At the same time, he wrote pieces that came from his heart. His dearly loved Josephine had passed away, and in her memory he composed Piano Sonata no. 31 in A-flat Major. In the first phrase, there's a sigh, a gentle melody, to which one could sing the words "Dear Josephine."

Dear Josephine. She would have to hear the Missa Solemnis and the Ninth Symphony from heaven.

The grand mass wasn't finished until 1823. In the first part, the Kyrie, Beethoven wrote the dedication: "For the heart, from the heart."

Beethoven wanted his music to awaken and strengthen spirituality within the listeners and singers, giving them a deep inner sense of God and his creative power. He hoped that this feeling would stay with people forever.

On May 7, 1824, in the Kärtnertor Theater, a "Large Musical Academy" was brought in to play Beethoven's works. Three pieces from nine masses were presented as "hymns" on the program, since religious works could not be played in public concert halls. The Ninth Symphony had its premiere. The audience cheered and cheered. Beethoven sulked, slouched in his seat, until finally the singer Caroline Unger bent down to him. She pulled him up and gently turned him toward the audience. At last, he could see their enthusiastic faces and clapping hands and understand the passionate reception his music had received. He bowed gratefully. Until that point, no applause had reached him in the depths of the silence that surrounded him.

Financially, however, the highly praised concert was not a success. The Prussian king, to whom the Ninth Symphony was dedicated, didn't send Beethoven the medals he desired, but instead, sent him an inexpensive ring. Beethoven was insulted and wanted to sell it immediately.

"Sell it?" cried the violinist Carl Holz angrily. He wrote to his deaf friend exactly what he thought: "But that is a present from a king!"

"Pah!" Beethoven answered. "I am a king, too."

BEETHOVEN SPENT THE SUMMER of 1825 in Baden, but when he thought about fall in Vienna, he decided to move back. He was enticed by the suburb of Alser. There was a former cloister for Spanish Benedictine monks there, which had become an apartment building.

Beethoven moved into a vacant apartment on the second floor. Five windows offered a marvelous view of the ramparts and towers of the city, all the way to St. Stephan's Cathedral. The front room, kitchen, and servant quarters opened directly into the courtyard. To the east one could see all the way to the Prater with its old trees. It was another bonus that his friend Stephan von Breuning lived in the area with his wife and son. And it was close to the Währinger Cemetery, where Josephine was buried.

He hung the portrait of his grandfather in the front room and crammed the piano next to the bed in the first bedroom. The workroom became the composition room, which led to the kitchen. Beethoven worked on his new string quartets, and he might have been quite comfortable in his new surroundings if only his health and his family had cooperated.

His worries about his nephew Karl tortured him more than any sickness ever would. Beethoven had tried so hard to take good care of him, but somehow his efforts went unrewarded. In the summer of 1826, Karl tried to commit suicide. Instead of finishing

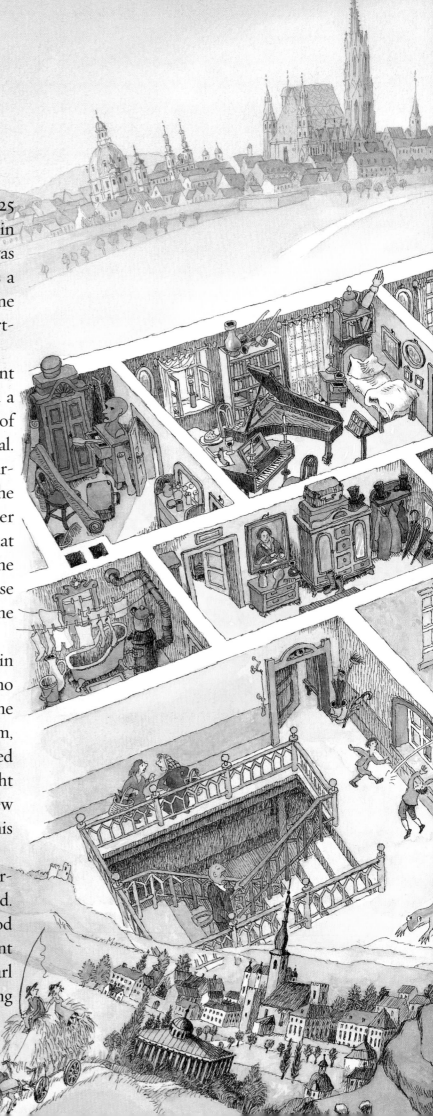

his exams at the Polytechnic University, he ran away, sold his watch, and bought a pistol with the proceeds. Near Baden, on the hill with the Rauhenstein ruins, Karl fired the pistol twice. Either he was a bad shot, or he was intentionally trying to miss. The second shot hit his head and Karl fell to the ground. A man driving a cart found him and brought him, at his request, to his mother in Vienna.

Karl was treated at a hospital, but because his injuries were the result of a suicide attempt, he was questioned by the authorities. Why did he want to die? Karl declared that he was a prisoner of his uncle's expectations. He wanted to be a soldier, but his uncle wouldn't let him. "I'm worse off because my uncle pushed me to be better," said Karl. Stephan von Breuning convinced Beethoven to give up the guardianship. Karl would need a good recommendation to get into the military after his suicide attempt. Von Breuning knew a Lieutenant Field Marshall, and when Beethoven dedicated his new string quartet in C-sharp Minor to him, Karl was allowed to join up as soon as his hair grew in over his head wound. Until then, Beethoven spent time with Karl at his brother Johann's country manor.

JOHANN MADE SURE that his brother was comfortable. He brought Beethoven the best wines while he polished the string quartets. Beethoven wrote letters that he'd meant to write for a long time—to his old friends Franz Wegeler and Leonore. Oh, Lorchen! Beethoven still carried her silhouette with him. He kept thinking of his time in Bonn. The things closest to his heart appeared in his music: reconciliation, peace, and joy.

Everyday life was a different matter. After the first few peaceful weeks, the family began to fight again. Beethoven boarded the first available coach with his nephew on December 1, wanting to return to Vienna. It was pouring rain, and an icy wind blew. They spent the night, frozen and wet, at a tavern in an unheated room. Beethoven arrived at his apartment shaking with chills and pneumonia. The doctor also diagnosed dropsy, and he had to repeatedly drain fluid from Beethoven's stomach. Beethoven bore these horrible intrusions with unbelievable patience. On top of everything, he also had jaundice, thanks to his weak liver.

During December, Karl lived with his uncle and took care of him. But by the beginning of 1827, he had to leave for the military. For once, there were no short-tempered words and no accusations as the uncle and nephew peacefully said good-bye to each other. In fact no one suffered anymore from Beethoven's insults. Not even the housekeeper, Sali. She even heard him say things like "thank you!" And "that was good!"

As long as he could, Beethoven continued to compose and write letters. These were the last days of his life. He rejoiced over every visit, every letter, every kind word, and every

handshake. Friends didn't abandon him and colleagues visited him. The Philharmonic Society of London sent money for his care. His former landlord, Baron von Pasqualati, had stewed cherries and peaches brought to him. Beethoven asked for specific types of wine. Laboriously he wrote short thank-you notes. "May heaven bless you for your loving help."

His publisher Schott in Mainz sent him a case of Rhine wine. "It's too bad," Beethoven whispered. "Too late . . ."

When the composer Hummel visited with his wife, Beethoven could no longer speak. Sweat beaded on his forehead. Mrs. Hummel took her fine batiste handkerchief and dried his face.

He thanked her with his eyes.

On March 26, 1827, in the late afternoon, there was a severe storm. Thunder pealed and lightning flashed through the snowy light. Loudly, lightning struck something nearby. Beethoven sat up one last time, balled his fist, and fell back onto the pillows, dead.

Twenty thousand people attended Beethoven's funeral at the Währinger Cemetery. The poet Franz Grillparzer wrote the eulogy, and the court actor Heinrich Anschütz recited it.

"He was an artist, but also a human being. A human being in the word's fullest meaning. But until his death he retained a humane heart toward all people, a fatherly one to his family, devoted his talent and life to the whole world!

So he was, so he died, so he shall live for all time."

❧ CHRONOLOGY ❧

1770	Ludwig van Beethoven is born in Bonn, Germany.
1773	Beethoven's grandfather dies December 24.
1774	Beethoven's brother Karl is born.
1776	Beethoven's brother Johann is born.
1778	Beethoven's first public concert.
1782/83	Beethoven's teacher, court organist Christian Gottlob Neefe, prints the 12-year-old's first compositions.
1784	The 14-year-old Beethoven is hired (and paid) as a musician by the court chapel in Bonn.
1785	Beethoven becomes the court organist.
1787	Beethoven's first trip to Vienna is cut short due to his mother's serious illness. He returns to Bonn quickly, and she dies July 17.
1789	Beethoven becomes his brothers' guardian. The French Revolution begins.
1792	Beethoven travels to Vienna for the second time to study with Haydn. His father dies in December.
1795	Beethoven's first public performance in Vienna is of his Piano Concerto in B-flat Major, op. 19.
1796	Concerts in Prague and Berlin. Starts having trouble with his hearing.
1799	Beethoven writes Piano Sonata no. 8 in C Minor: *Pathétique*, op. 13.
1800	Premiere of Beethoven's First Symphony in C Major, op. 21, at his first solo concert.
1801	Beethoven's first String Quartet no. 6 in B-flat Major, op. 18, is printed.
1802	Beethoven's Piano Sonata No. 14 in C-sharp Minor: *Moonlight Sonata*, op. 27, is printed. In October, Beethoven writes his will in the Viennese suburb of Heiligenstadt.
1803	Beethoven works on *Eroica*. He teaches the Archduke Rudolph (piano and composition).
1804	Beethoven works on his opera *Leonore* (later called *Fidelio*). *Eroica* has a private premiere. Napoleon becomes the emperor of France, Beethoven rips up the dedication of *Eroica* to Napoleon.
1805	French troops occupy Vienna. *Leonore* (later called *Fidelio*) premieres to an almost empty house.
1806	Beethoven writes his first Concerto for Violin and Orchestra in D Major, op. 61.
1808	On December 22 Beethoven premieres parts of the Mass in C Major, and Symphony no. 5 in C Minor, op. 67, and Symphony no. 6 in F Major: *Pastorale*, op. 68.
1809	Haydn dies. Beethoven receives an annual salary from the Archduke Rudolph and the princes Lobkowitz and Kinsky.
1810	Beethoven composes music for Goethe's *Egmont*. He meets Bettina von Brentano. He falls in love with the young Therese Malfatti. The title of the piece that he dedicated to her—*Für Therese*—was later erroneously read as *Für Elise*.
1811	Beethoven works on Symphony no. 7 in A Major, op. 92, and Symphony no. 8 in F Major, op. 93.
1812	Beethoven meets Goethe several times in the Bohemian spa town of Teplitz. He writes the famous letter to his "Immortal Beloved."
1813	After Napoleon's defeat Beethoven writes his battle symphony: *Wellingtons Sieg, oder die Schlacht bei Vittoria* (Wellington's Victory, or the Battle of Vittoria), op. 91, which opens to huge public success.
1814	Beethoven revises his opera and calls it *Fidelio*. At the time of the Vienna Convention, he's at the peak of his fame.
1816	After the death of his brother, Kaspar Karl, Beethoven becomes guardian of his nephew, Karl. He composes the song cycle: "An die ferne Geliebte" (To the Distant Beloved), op. 98.
1817	Despite progressive deafness Beethoven conducts his Eighth Symphony in concert.
1818	Beethoven composes the Piano Sonata no. 29 in B-flat Major: *Hammerklavier-Sonate*, op. 106. He loses his hearing entirely, and in order to speak to him, "conversation notebooks" must be used.
1819	Beethoven begins composing his Mass in D major: *Missa Solemnis*, op. 123.
1821	Countess Josephine dies. In her memory Beethoven writes the Piano Sonata no. 31 in A-flat Major, op. 110.
1823	World premiere of the *Missa Solemnis* in St. Petersburg. Beethoven works on his Ninth Symphony, op. 125.
1824	On May 7, Beethoven's Ninth Symphony, op. 125, has its premiere in the Kärntnertor Theater with the final chorus set to Schiller's "Ode to Joy." Beethoven can only see—not hear—the thunderous applause.
1826	Beethoven finishes his last string quartets. His nephew, Karl, attempts suicide. After a visit with his brother, Johann, at his country estate, Beethoven returns to Vienna with severe pneumonia. He does not recover.
1827	Beethoven names his nephew, Karl, as his primary heir. March 26th, Beethoven dies in his apartment in Vienna. March 29th, he is buried in the Währinger Cemetery.